T0354992

The Doctor Says: But GOD Says:

The Doctor Says: But GOD Says:

Gary R. Granato

THE DOCTOR SAYS: BUT GOD SAYS:

iUniverse books may be ordered through booksellers or by contacting:

iUniverse
1663 Liberty Drive
Bloomington, IN 47403
www.iuniverse.com
844-349-9409

ISBN: 978-1-6632-6429-9 (sc)
ISBN: 978-1-6632-6430-5 (e)

Library of Congress Control Number: 2024912912

Print information available on the last page.

iUniverse rev. date: 06/28/2024

Have your **BIBLE** at your side as you read this research.

Look up every verse in your **BIBLE** that you read.

Spend at least five minutes meditating on each verse.

Picture **GOD** working each verse for your good in your imagination.

Speak each verse out loud.

Speak each verse over yourself.

You can fill in "*The Doctor Says*:" on every page with anything a doctor might have said to you.

Don't deny the facts; but live in the reality that **GOD** can change the facts.

Take a verse and write it down on a 3x5 card and carry it around with you all day and meditate on it.

I felt like I had been sent to death row, that it was all over for me. As it turned out, it was the best thing that could have happened. Instead of trusting in my own strength or wits to get out of it, I was forced to trust **GOD** totally – not a bad idea since HE's the **GOD** who raises the dead!

2 Corinthians 1:9 (Message)

And without faith it is impossible to please HIM, for whoever would draw near to **GOD** must believe that HE exists and that HE rewards those who seek HIM.

Hebrews 11:6 (ESV)

Since we have the same spirit of faith according to what has been written, "I believed, and so I spoke," we also believe, and so we also speak.

2 Corinthians 4:13 (ESV)

The doctor says:

All of our options have been exhausted.

But GOD says:

Meditate on MY WORD day and night.

Psalm 1:2 (ESV)

I AM amused at his presumption.

Psalm 2:4 (Message)

I will leave this enemy powerless to harm you.

Psalm 3:7

I will vindicate you. I will free you from affliction.

Psalm 4:1 (HCSB)

You are MY Temple (house), and MY SPIRIT lives in this house – in you.

1 Corinthians 3:16 (LB)

No wicked can dwell with ME.

Psalm 5:4 (NIV)

- Gary R. Granato -

The doctor says:

Be prepared for the worst.

But GOD says:

I AM not displeased with you. Let's just get that cleared up right from the start.

Psalm 6:1 (KJV)

I AM you refuge, you can trust ME; I will deliver you from the worst.

Psalm 7:1 (AMP)

I will put all of your diseases under MY feet.

1 Corinthians 15:25 (ESV)

MY enemies turn back; they stumble and perish within you.

Psalm 9 verse 3 (NIV)

I AM not far away. The enemy knows I AM here.

Psalm 10:1 (MEV)

The doctor says:

The cancer is spreading

But GOD says:

I AM aware of what's going on.

Psalm 11:4 (AMP)

MY WORDS are pure WORDS: purified seven times.

Psalm 12:6 (KJV)

I have not forgotten you. I AM looking right at the enemy now.

Psalm 13:1 (TLB)

I AM with you who are righteous. I AM your refuge.

Psalm 14:5+6 (HCSB)

I AM before you; I AM at your right hand, do not be troubled.

Acts 2:25 (TEV)

The doctor says:

This disease is uncurable.

But GOD says:

I will keep you safe. You are firmly formed. I have your feet on the life path.

Psalm 16:1,9+11 (Message)

I AM your steadfast love. I will keep you as the apple of MY eye; hiding you in the shadow of MY wings.

Psalm 17:7+8 (ESV)

I love you, I AM your strength.

Psalm 18:1 (ESV)

MY reputation is a lifetime guarantee. MY decisions are accurate.

Psalm 19:9 (Message)

I know when you are in trouble! I AM your protection!

Psalm 20:1 (TEV)

The doctor says:

Everybody gets old and feeble.

But GOD says:

You will find joy in MY strength! You will rejoice in MY victory!

Psalm 21:2 (HCSB)

You will never be disappointed when you seek MY aid.

Psalm 22:5 (TLB)

Fear no evil: for I AM with you; I will comfort you.

Psalm 23:4 (KJV)

I gave you righteousness and salvation.

Psalm 24:5 (AMP)

Trust in ME; you won't be ashamed; the enemy will not triumph over you.

Psalm 25:2 (MEV)

The doctor says:

Fatigue will be a side effect.

But GOD says:

Trust in ME without wavering.

Psalm 26:1 (NIV)

I AM your light and your salvation.

Psalm 27:1 (NIV)

I always hear you. I will destroy your enemy and trip them down and out.

Psalm 28:2+5 (MEV)

MY voice breaks cedars; yes, breaks in pieces the cedars of Lebanon.

Psalm 29:5 (AMP)

I will save you from your enemy. I will refuse to let the enemy triumph over you.

Psalm 30:1 (TLB)

The doctor says:

Get your affairs in order.

But GOD says:

I would never let you be put to shame, I will deliver you!

Psalm 31:1 (ESV)

I AM your hiding place; I will preserve you from trouble; I will surround you with deliverance.

Psalm 32:7 (KJV)

MY WORD is solid to the core; I make everything sound inside and out.

Psalm 33:4

The oppressed look to ME and are glad; they will never be disappointed.

Psalm 34:5

The doctor says:

Humanly speaking, this is impossible.

But GOD says:

I will fight those who fight you.

Psalm 35:1 (HCSB)

I will feed you with blessings from MY own table and let you drink rivers of delight.

Psalm 36:8 (TLB)

The enemy will be cut down like grass, and wither as the green herb.

Psalm 37:2 (AMP)

I will not abandon you, I will not be far from you.

Psalm 38:21 (MEV)

I will set your feet on a rock and give you a firm place to stand.

Psalm 40:2 (NIV)

The doctor says:

I can't help you anymore.

But GOD says:

I will deliver you in your time of trouble.

Psalm 41:1 (NIV)

I will command MY lovingkindness in the daytime, and in the night MY song will be with you.

Psalm 42:8 (MEV)

I AM the GOD of your strength – your STRONGHOLD – in whom you can take refuge.

Psalm 43:2 (AMP)

I AM your KING and your GOD. I speak victory for you over the enemy.

Psalm 44:4 (TLB)

The doctor says:

It's just a matter of time now.

But GOD says:

I will anoint you with the oil of joy.

Psalm 45:7 (HCSB)

I AM your shelter and strength, always ready to help in times of trouble.

Psalm 46:1 (TEV)

I AM with you.

Matthew 1:23 (ESV)

I AM your fortress.

Psalm 48 verse 3 (ESV)

I will snatch you from the clutch of death, I will reach down and grab you.

Psalm 49:15 (Message)

The doctor says:

Just hope for the best.

But GOD says:

I will deliver you, and you shall glorify ME.

Psalm 50:15 (KJV)

I AM your deliverer from evil.

Matthew 6:13 (KJV)

I will sweep up the enemy and throw him out, pull him up by the roots.

Psalm 52:5 (Message)

I will command MY angels concerning you, to guard you.

Luke 4:10 (ESV)

- Gary R. Granato -

The doctor says:

Know we are doing everything we can.

But GOD says:

I will save you by MY Name, and vindicate you by MY might.

Psalm 54:1 (ESV)

Leave your troubles with ME, I will defend you.

Psalm 55:22 (TEV)

The enemy will retreat. Know this: I AM for you.

Psalm 56:9 (HCSB)

I will send down help from heaven to save you, because of MY love and MY faithfulness toward you.

Psalm 57 verse 3 (TLB)

You are more than a conquer, through ME who loves you.

Romans 8:37 (AMP)

The doctor says:

Little can be done.

But GOD says:

I will deliver you from the enemy; I AM your refuge from those who rise up against you.

Psalm 59:1 (MEV)

I will restore you!

Psalm 60:1 (NIV)

I AM a shelter and a refuge for you, a strong tower against the adversary.

Psalm 61 verse 3 (AMP)

From ME comes your salvation.

Psalm 62:1 (KJV)

You will see MY strength and glory.

Psalm 63:2 (TLB)

The doctor says:

Meager chance that it will work.

But GOD says:

I will protect your life from the terror of the enemy.

Psalm 64:1 (HCSB)

I will give you victory, I will do wonderful things to save you.

Psalm 65:5 (TEV)

So great is MY power that MY enemies come cringing to ME.

Psalm 66 verse 3 (ESV)

I AM your power, and glory, forever.

Matthew 6:13 (KJV)

One look at ME and the wicked vanish.

Psalm 68:2 (Message)

The doctor says:

Nobody has survived this before.

But GOD says:

Now is the acceptable time: now is the multitude of MY mercy, now is the truth of MY salvation.

Psalm 69:13 (KJV)

The enemy who is trying to kill you will be defeated and confused.

Psalm 70:2 (TEV)

I AM you refuge; I will never disgrace you.

Psalm 71:1 (HCSB)

I will defend you and crush your oppressors.

Psalm 72:4 (TLB)

- Gary R. Granato -

The doctor says:

Only a few hours to go before death.

But GOD says:

Nevertheless I AM continually with you, I do hold you in MY right hand.

Psalm 73:23 (AMP)

I AM, KING; I bring salvation.

Psalm 74:12 (NIV)

For your eyes will see MY salvation.

Luke 2:30 (KJV)

At MY rebuke, the enemy will lay stunned.

Psalm 76:6 (MEV)

I AM the GOD who can do wonders; I will declare MY strength.

Psalm 77:14 (MEV)

The doctor says:

Permanent damage

But GOD says:

Believe in ME and trust MY deliverance.

Psalm 78:22 (NIV)

MY compassion and tender mercy will speedily come to meet you.

Psalm 79:8 (AMP)

I will display MY power and radiant glory.

Psalm 80:1 (TLB)

I will relieve your shoulder from the burden.

Psalm 81:6 (HCSB)

I AM the power to heal sicknesses, and to cast out devils.

Mark 3:15 (KJV)

- Gary R. Granato -

The doctor says:

Quick decline is possible.

But GOD says:

I will scatter away the enemy like dust, like straw blown away by the wind.

Psalm 83:13 (TEV)

Blessed are you whose strength is in ME.

Psalm 84:5 (ESV)

I will give you the salvation you need!

Psalm 85:7 (Message)

I AM mercy; I give strength.

Psalm 86:16 (KJV)

I will take you by your right hand, and lift you up; you will receive strength.

Acts 3:7 (KJV)

The doctor says:

Really hard disease to control.

But GOD says:

I AM more powerful than your troubles; you will not die.

Psalm 88 verse 3 (Message)

I scatter the enemy with MY mighty arm.

Psalm 89:10 (ESV)

I will redeem you with MY stretched out arm.

Exodus 6:6

I AM your defender and protector. I AM your GOD; trust in ME.

Psalm 91:2

I will make you rejoice.

Psalm 92:4

- Gary R. Granato -

The doctor says:

Sadly, we have hit a brick wall.

But GOD says:

I AM KING! I AM robed with majesty and strength.

Psalm 93:1 (TLB)

MY mercy and lovingkindness will hold you up.

Psalm 94:18 (AMP)

I AM your Rock of salvation.

Psalm 95:1

I AM salvation, and strength: for the accuser is cast down.

Revelation 12:10 (KJV)

I will set everything right.

Psalm 97:6 (Message)

The doctor says:

This is your last option.

But GOD says:

I should have been your first option.

I will make known MY salvation to you.

Psalm 98:2 (ESV)

I will give you the victory through JESUS.

1 Corinthians 15:57 (KJV)

I AM good; MY mercy is everlasting.

Psalm 100:5 (KJV)

Be strong in the strength of MY might.

Ephesians 6:10 (ESV)

- Gary R. Granato -

The doctor says:

Understand the gravity of the situation.

But GOD says:

MY SPIRIT in you is far stronger than anything in the world.

1 John 4:4 (ESV)

I forgave all your sins and heal all your diseases.

Psalm 103 verse 3 (ESV)

You are made fit by the once-for-all sacrifice of JESUS.

Hebrews 10:10 (Message)

I will make you stronger than the enemy.

Psalm 105:24 (ESV)

The doctor says:

Very hard to contain this type of infection.

But GOD says:

I will save you for MY Name's sake, to make MY mighty power known.

Psalm 106:8 (NIV)

I will redeem you from the hand of the enemy.

Psalm 107:2 (MEV)

I will deliver you: I will save you with MY right hand.

Psalm 108:6 (KJV)

I will act for you for MY Name's sake; because MY mercy and lovingkindness are good, I will deliver you.

Psalm 109:21 (AMP)

The doctor says:

We tried everything we know how to do.

But GOD says:

For with ME nothing shall be impossible.

Luke 1:37 (KJV)

I will subdue your enemies and make them bow low before you.

Psalm 110:1 (TLB)

MY works are great, studied by all who delight in them.

Psalm 111:2 (HCSB)

Do not be afraid of receiving bad news; keep the faith, trust in ME.

Psalm 112:7 (TEV)

The doctor says:

Anemia

But GOD says:

I AM higher than anything and anyone.

Psalm 113:4

Let your faith rest in MY power.

1 Corinthians 2:5 (ESV)

Trust in ME, I will help you and protect you.

Psalm 115:9 (TEV)

I AM gracious and righteous; I AM compassionate.

Psalm 116:5 (HCSB)

I reward those who sincerely look for ME.

Hebrews 11:6 (TLB)

- Gary R. Granato -

The doctor says:

Bipolar Disorder

But GOD says:

I will set you free and in a large place.

Psalm 118:5 (AMP)

I will deal bountifully with you, that you may live, and keep MY WORD.

Psalm 119:17

I AM good, a stronghold in a day of distress.

Nahum 1:7 (MEV)

I watch over you – I AM your shade at your right hand.

Psalm 121:5 (NIV)

I AM your "Peace be within you".

Psalm 122:8 (ESV)

The doctor says:

Cerebral Palsy

But GOD says:

I will never let you down, never walk off and leave you.

Hebrews 13:5 (Message)

Your help is in the Name of the LORD, who made heaven and earth.

Psalm 124:8 (ESV)

I AM round about you forever.

Psalm 125:2 (KJV)

I will do great things for you.

Psalm 126:2 (NIV)

Believe in ME, and you shall be established; believe MY prophets, and you will prosper.

2 Chronicles 20:20 (KJV)

- Gary R. Granato -

The doctor says:

Diabetes

But GOD says:

You will be happy, and it shall be well with you.

Psalm 128:2 (MEV)

The enemy might have afflicted you, yet he will not prevail against you.

Psalm 129:1+2 (AMP)

Trust ME to help, for I have promised.

Psalm 130:5

Put your hope in ME, both now and forever.

Psalm 131 verse 3 (HCSB)

The doctor says:

Erectile Dysfunction

But GOD says:

You will succeed, because I AM able to make you succeed.

Romans 14:4 (TEV)

I give radiant health and happiness.

Zechariah 9:17 (ESV)

I will heal you, lead you, and comfort you.

Isaiah 57:18 (Message)

- Gary R. Granato -

The doctor says:

Fecal Incontinence

But GOD says:

I will be healing for your body and strengthening for your bones.

Proverbs 3:8 (HCSB)

MY promises are backed by all the honor of MY Name.

Psalm 138:2

I AM behind and before you, I have laid MY hand upon you.

Psalm 139:5 (AMP)

I will preserve you from the violent enemy who have planned to overthrow you.

Psalm 140:4

The doctor says:

Gangrene

But GOD says:

I will heal you: I will lead you also and restore your comfort.

Isaiah 57:18 (KJV)

I AM your refuge; I care for your life.

Psalm 142:4 (NIV)

I have a steadfast love for you, I will make known the way you should go.

Psalm 143:8 (ESV)

I AM the bedrock in which you stand, I will lay your enemy low.

Psalm 144:1+2 (Message)

I AM good to all, and MY mercy is over all that I have made.

Psalm 145:9

The doctor says:

Hepatitis

But GOD says:

I give power to the faint; and to them who have no might I increase strength.

Isaiah 40:29 (KJV)

Put your hope in MY unfailing love.

Psalm 33:18 (KJV)

I will heal your broken heart, I will bind up your wounds.

Psalm 147 verse 3 (MEV)

Death and life are in the power of the tongue.

Proverbs 18:21 (AMP)

The doctor says:

Inflammatory Bowel Disease

But GOD says:

I will give you renewed health and vitality.

Proverbs 3:8 (TLB)

I AM good, a stronghold in a day of distress.

Nahum 1:7 (HCSB)

I will guide and protect you.

Psalm 1:6 (TEV)

I will break the enemy with a rod of iron and dash him in pieces like a potter's vessel.

Psalm 2:9 (ESV)

I will shield you on all sides; I will lift your head high.

Psalm 3 verse 3 (Message)

The doctor says:

Jaundice

But GOD says:

I alone will make you dwell in safety and confident trust.

Psalm 4:8 (AMP)

I AM your refuge; I will defend you.

Psalm 5:11 (MEV)

I will have mercy on you, I will heal you.

Psalm 6:2 (KJV)

I AM your refuge; I will save and deliver you from the enemy.

Psalm 7:1

I will keep you safe and secure from the enemy.

Psalm 8:2 (ESV)

The doctor says:

Kidney Stones

But GOD says:

I will make your enemies retreat, they will stumble and perish before you.

Psalm 9 verse 3 (HCSB)

I will break the enemy. I will go after them until the last of them is destroyed.

Psalm 10:15 (TLB)

By MY strength I will bring you out of bondage.

Exodus 13:14 (AMP)

I will protect you from the enemy who maligns you.

Psalm 12:5 (NIV)

The enemy will not loom over you.

Psalm 13:2 (MEV)

- Gary R. Granato -

The doctor says:

Lupus

But GOD says:

I will bandage your wounds, pouring on olive oil and wine. I will take care of you.

Luke 10:34 (HCSB)

I always do what I promise, no matter how much it may cost.

Psalm 15:4 (TEV)

I AM your refuge. I AM your help.

Psalm 16:1+2 (TLB)

I will keep you as the apple of MY eye, I will hide you under the shadow of MY wings.

Psalm 17:8 (KJV)

I AM your strength, your rock, your fortress, and your deliverer.

Psalm 18:1+2 (ESV)

The doctor says:

Meningitis

But GOD says:

MY WORD is better.

Psalm 19:10 (Message)

I will answer you in the day of trouble! MY Name will protect you!

Psalm 20:1 (ESV)

You will joy in MY strength, and in MY salvation how greatly you will rejoice!

Psalm 21:1 (KJV)

I will never forsake you. I will never refuse to help you.

Psalm 22:1 (TLB)

I will renew your life; I will lead you along the right paths for MY Name's sake.

Psalm 23 verse 3 (HCSB)

- Gary R. Granato -

The doctor says:

Narcolepsy

But GOD says:

I AM the LORD, strong and mighty, the LORD, victorious in battle.

Psalm 24:8 (TEV)

I will lead you in MY truth and teach you, for I AM GOD of you salvation.

Psalm 25:5 (MEV)

MY love is ever before you.

Psalm 26 verse 3 (NIV)

I AM your light and your salvation.

Psalm 27:1 (AMP)

I will not turn a deaf ear when you call to ME.

Psalm 28:1 (Message)

I AM your glory and strength.

Psalm 29:1 (ESV)

The doctor says:

Osteoporosis

But GOD says:

I will lift you up, I will not have the enemy to rejoice over you.

Psalm 30:1 (KJV)

You can trust in ME, I AM your refuge; you will never be disappointed in ME; I will deliver you.

Psalm 31:1 (AMP)

Do not keep silent regarding MY promises and your bones will not waste away.

Psalm 32 verse 3 (NIV)

MY WORD is upright, all MY work is done in truth.

Psalm 33:4 (MEV)

The doctor says:

Parkinson's

But GOD says:

You will praise ME for what I AM going to do; all who are oppressed listen and be glad.

Psalm 34:2 (TEV)

I will shield you – I will come to your aid.

Psalm 35:2 (HCSB)

MY steadfast love is as great as the heavens. MY faithfulness reaches beyond the clouds.

Psalm 36:5 (TLB)

Delight yourself in ME, and I will give you the desires of your heart.

Psalm 37:4 (ESV)

The doctor says:

Quadriceps Tendon Rupture

But GOD says:

I will not dump you, I will stand you up. I will help you; I will give you some wide open space in your life!

Psalm 38:21+22 (Message)

Believe in MY healing power, and you will be established; believe MY prophets, and you will succeed.

2 Chronicles 20:20 (ESV)

Wait patiently for ME to help you; I will lift you up out of your pit of despair, I will set your feet on a hard, firm path and steady you as you walk along.

Psalm 40:1+2 (TLB)

I will not give you over to the desire of the enemy.

Psalm 41:2 (HCSB)

The doctor says:

Rapid Heartbeat

But GOD says:

Turn your thoughts to ME when your heart is breaking.

Psalm 42:6 (TEV)

I have not rejected you; I AM the GOD of your refuge.

Psalm 43:2 (MEV)

With MY hand I will drive out the enemy and firmly plant you; I will crush the enemy and make you flourish.

Psalm 44:2 (NIV)

MY right hand will guide you to tremendous things.

Psalm 45:4 (AMP)

The doctor says:

Schizophrenia

But GOD says:

I AM your refuge and strength, a very present help in trouble.

Psalm 46:1 (KJV)

I will keep you in perfect peace when your mind is stayed on ME.

Isaiah 26 verse 3 (ESV)

Call the church elders together to pray for you and anoint you with oil in the Name of JESUS. Believing – prayer will heal you.

James 5:14 (Message)

I will redeem you from the power of the enemy.

Psalm 49:15 (AMP)

Yes, call upon ME in the day of trouble; I will deliver you, and you will honor ME.

Psalm 50:15 (ESV)

- Gary R. Granato -

The doctor says:

Tinnitus

But GOD says:

I will turn your life around.

Psalm 53:6 (Message)

I will supply every need of yours.

Philippians 4:19 (ESV)

I AM your help; I AM the ONE who will sustain you.

Psalm 54:4 (NIV)

Do not be distracted by the noise of the enemy. I AM your shelter from the stormy wind and tempest.

Psalm 55 verses 3 and 8 (AMP)

In the day you are afraid, trust in ME.

Psalm 56 verse 3 (MEV)

The doctor says:

Ulcer

But GOD says:

In the shadow of MY wings make your refuge.

Psalm 57:1 (KJV)

I AM like good medicine, healing your wounds and easing your pains.

Proverbs 3:8 (TEV)

I will deliver you from the enemy, I will protect you from those who rise up against you.

Psalm 59:1 (HCSB)

I AM your defense; I will never desert you. You are one of MY favorites.

Psalm 60:1 (TLB)

I AM your refuge, a strong tower against the enemy.

Psalm 61 verse 3 (ESV)

The doctor says:

Vascular Dementia

But GOD says:

I AM a solid rock under your feet, breathing room for your soul.

Psalm 62:2 (Message)

I will be your help, in the shadow of MY wings you will rejoice.

Psalm 63:7 (KJV)

I will guard your life from the dread of the enemy.

Psalm 64:1 (MEV)

For MY SPIRIT in you is far stronger than anything in the world.

1 John 4:4 (Message)

So great is MY power that the enemy comes cringing to ME.

Psalm 66 verse 3 (ESV)

The doctor says:

West Nile Virus

But GOD says:

I will be gracious to you and bless you and make MY face shine upon you.

Psalm 67:1 (NIV)

I will arise in you, and the enemy will scatter; he will flee before ME.

Psalm 68:1 (AMP)

I AM always ready to give you a plentiful supply of love and kindness.

Psalm 69:13 (TLB)

I will deliver you. I will hurry to help you.

Psalm 70:1 (HCSB)

I AM your protection; I will never let you be defeated.

Psalm 71:1 (TEV)

The doctor says:

X Y or Z

But GOD says:

I will defend your cause, give deliverance and crush the oppressor!

Psalm 72:4 (ESV)

I will wisely and tenderly lead you, and then I will bless you.

Psalm 73:24 (Message)

With MY mighty strength I smash the heads of the enemy.

Psalm 74:13 (TEV)

I will break forth upon the enemy.

2 Samuel 5:20 (KJV)

I shatter flaming arrows, the sword, and all the weapons of the enemy.

Psalm 76 verse 3 (HCSB)

And GOD Continues To Say:

I will never reject you. I will always be favorable towards you.

Psalm 77:7 (TLB)

Set your hope in ME and do not forget the works that I have done.

Psalm 78:7 (AMP)

I will help you for the glory of MY Name; I will deliver you.

Psalm 79:9 (NIV)

I will stir up MY strength, and come and rescue you.

Psalm 80:2 (MEV)

I AM your strength!

Psalm 81:1 (ESV)

I AM here to defend you, to stand up for you.

Psalm 82:4 (Message)

- Gary R. Granato -

GOD Continues With HIS Promises

I will shut up your defiling, demonic spirits and send them packing.

Mark 1:28 (Message)

You will go from MY strength to even more of MY strength.

Psalm 84:7 (MEV)

I will restore you again.

Psalm 85:4 (NIV)

I will preserve your life because you trust in ME.

Psalm 86:2 (ESV)

I AM with you, I will take your hand and raise you up also.

Mark 1:31 (Message)

GOD continues with HIS promises:

I will stand up to your troubles and chase them away.

Psalm 88 verse 3 (TLB)

You will sing about MY faithful love forever.

Psalm 89:1 (HCSB)

I will satisfy you early with MY mercy; that you may rejoice and be glad.

Psalm 90:14 (KJV)

You dwell in MY shelter and will rest in MY shadow.

Psalm 91:1 (NIV)

I will show you MY lovingkindness in the morning, and faithfulness in the night.

Psalm 92:2 (MEV)

I reign, I AM girded with strength and power.

Psalm 93:1 (AMP)

GODS Love Continues:

I will give you rest from days of trouble.

Psalm 94:13 (TEV)

I will cure your sick body and tormented spirit also.

Mark 1:33 (Message)

You will show off MY salvation from day to day.

Psalm 96:2 (KJV)

Fire goes before ME and burns up MY foes on every side.

Psalm 97 verse 3 (HCSB)

I will roll up MY sleeves, I will set things right.

Psalm 98:1 (Message)

I will throw out this demon also.

Mark 1:39 (Message)

GOD Continues On:

For MY WORDS will certainly come true at the proper time.

Luke 1:20 (TLB)

For I AM going to wonderfully bless you also.

Luke 1:30 (TLB)

I will not hide MY face from you in your day of trouble. I will listen closely to you; I will answer you quickly.

Psalm 102:2 (HCSB)

I forgave all your iniquities; I healed all your diseases.

Psalm 103 verse 3 (KJV)

Your gladness will come from ME.

Psalm 104:34 (TEV)

- Gary R. Granato -

GOD Continues To Speak:

I AM mindful of MY covenant for it is forever imprinted on MY heart.

Psalm 105:8 (AMP)

I will remember you, when I give out MY favor; I will deliver you with MY deliverance.

Psalm 106:4 (MEV)

I will redeem you from the hand of the foe.

Psalm 107:2 (NIV)

For every one of MY promises shall surely come true.

Luke 1:37 (TLB)

I will deal on your behalf for MY Name's sake; because MY steadfast love is good I will deliver you.

Psalm 109:21 (ESV)

I gave you MY WORD and I won't take it back.

Psalm 110:4 (Message)

More Promises From GOD:

For I, the mighty HOLY ONE, will do great things for you.

Luke 1:49 (TLB)

Do not be afraid of receiving bad news; be strong in faith, trusting ME.

Psalm 112:7 (TEV)

I will give light to you who sit in darkness and death's shadow, I will guide you to the path of peace.

Luke 1:79 (TLB)

In ME is life.

John 1:4 (KJV)

I AM your help and shield.

Psalm 115:9 (HCSB)

I AM gracious and righteous; I AM full of compassion.

Psalm 116:5 (NIV)

More Of GODS Benefits and Gifts:

MY merciful kindness is great towards you, and MY faithfulness endures forever.

Psalm 117:2 (MEV)

I AM on your side, I AM among those who help you; you shall see your desire established upon the enemy.

Psalm 118:7 (AMP)

I will deal bountifully with you, that you may live and keep MY WORD.

Psalm 119:17 (ESV)

I MYSELF are right alongside you to keep you steady and on track.

1 Corinthians 1:8 (Message)

I will come and help you, who made heaven and earth.

Psalm 121:2 (KJV)

All the gifts and benefits that come from ME are yours.

1 Corinthians 1 verse 3 (Message)

GOD Continues The Comfort:

I will show you favor.

Psalm 123:2 (HCSB)

I will not let the enemy devour you.

Psalm 124:6 (TLB)

As the mountains surround Jerusalem, I will surround you, now and forever.

Psalm 125:2 (TEV)

I will do great things for you.

Psalm 126:2 (AMP)

I AM the GOD of all comfort, I will comfort you in this tribulation.

2 Corinthians 1 verses 3+4 (MEV)

I will deliver you also.

2 Corinthians 1:10

The enemy will not gain the victory over you.

Psalm 129:2 (NIV)

GODS Confidence Continues:

I always listen when you call for help.

Psalm 130:2 (TEV)

In ME is "Yes".

2 Corinthians 1:19+20 (MEV)

Surely I will never go back on a promise.

Psalm 132:11 (TLB)

I will rescue you from this present evil enemy.

Galatians 1:4 (HCSB)

Be confident of this very thing, that I who has begun a good work in you will perform it until the day of JESUS CHRIST.

Philippians 1:6 (KJV)

I will deliver you from the power of darkness.

Colossians 1:13 (KJV)

GODS Life Giving WORD Continues:

I will rescue you from your foes.

Psalm 136:24 (HCSB)

I consider it just when I afflict the enemy who afflicts you.

2 Thessalonians 1:6 (ESV)

Call to ME, I will step in; I will make your life large with strength.

Psalm 138 verse 3 (Message)

MY hand will lead you, MY right hand shall hold you.

Psalm 139:10 (AMP)

I will rescue you from the enemy; I will protect you.

Psalm 140:1 (NIV)

I will guard your mouth; I will keep watch over the door of your lips. Because death and life are in the power of the tongue.

Psalm 141 verse 3 and Proverbs 18:21 (MEV)

GODS faithful forever WORDS continue:

I AM your refuge and portion.

Psalm 142:5 (KJV)

I AM faithful to MY promises.

Psalm 143:1 (TLB)

I AM your protector and defender, your shelter and SAVIOR, your safety. I will subdue the enemy under you.

Psalm 144:2 (TEV)

I AM gracious and full of compassion, and great in mercy, slow to anger.

Psalm 145:8 (MEV)

I AM maker of heaven and earth, the sea – and everything in them – I will remain faithful to you forever.

Psalm 146:6 (NIV)

I heal the brokenhearted and bind up their wounds.

Psalm 147 verse 3 (NIV)

GODS encouragement continues:

I will grant you the needed strength.

1 Timothy 1:12 (AMP)

I take pleasure in you; I will honor you with victory.

Psalm 149:4 (TEV)

I will shower you with MY kindness, mercy and peace.

2 Timothy 1:2 (TLB)

I will give you strength in suffering.

2 Timothy 1:8 (TLB)

I will break the enemy with a rod of iron; I will dash them to pieces like a potter's vessel.

Psalm 2:9 (KJV)

I AM a shield around you, your glory, I will lift up your head.

Psalm 3 verse 3 (HCSB)

GODS Presence Continues:

I will show MY love and kindness to you.

2 Timothy 1:9 (TLB)

Take refuge in ME, put your trust in ME, and rejoice.

Psalm 5:11 (AMP)

I will turn and deliver you; I will save you because of MY unfailing love.

Psalm 6:4 (NIV)

I will save you from the enemy who is persecuting you, I will deliver you.

Psalm 7:1

I will remember you, I will look after you.

Psalm 8:4 (HCSB)

I will turn back the enemy, they shall fall and perish at MY presence.

Psalm 9 verse 3

GOD continues with HIS powerful WORD:

I will punish the wicked enemy! I will remember you who is suffering!

Psalm 10:12 (TEV)

I have broken the power of death and will show you the way of everlasting life by trusting ME.

2 Timothy 1:10 (TLB)

I will place you in safety in which you belong.

Psalm 12:5 (ESV)

You will look life right in the eye, the enemy will not get the best of you.

Psalm 13:4 (Message)

I sustain all things by MY powerful WORD.

Hebrews 1 verse 3 (NIV)

I will anoint you with the oil of joy.

Hebrews 1:9 (NIV)

GOD continues to defend you:

I will preserve you, for in ME you have refuge.

Psalm 16:1 (MEV)

I will keep and guard you as the pupil of MY eye; I will hide you in the shadow of MY wings.

Psalm 17:8 (AMP)

I AM your fort where you can enter and be safe; no enemy can follow you in.

Psalm 18:2 (TLB)

I AM your refuge and your redeemer.

Psalm 19:14 (TEV)

I hear you in your day of trouble; I will defend you.

Psalm 20:1 (KJV)

MY hand will capture all your enemies; MY right hand will seize those who hate you.

Psalm 21:8 (HCSB)

GODS Grace Continues:

I will deliver you; I will rescue you, for I delight in you!

Psalm 22:8 (ESV)

I will let you catch your breath and send you in the right direction.

Psalm 23 verse 3 (Message)

I AM strong and mighty, the LORD mighty in battle.

Psalm 24:8 (AMP)

I will watch over your life and deliver you! I AM your refuge.

Psalm 25:20 (MEV)

I will redeem you and be gracious to you.

Psalm 26:11 (HCSB)

I AM your light and your salvation; I AM the strength of your life.

Psalm 27:1 (KJV)

GODS Love For You Continues:

I will protect and defend you; I will give you help and make you glad.

Psalm 28:7 (TEV)

I will bless you with much mercy and much peace.

2 John 3 (TLB)

O LORD my GOD, I called to you for help and YOU healed ME.

Psalm 30:2 (NIV)

MY granite cave a hiding place, MY high cliff aerie a place of safety.

Psalm 31:2 (Message)

I AM your hiding place; I preserve you from trouble; I surround you with shouts of deliverance.

Psalm 32:7 (ESV)

Put your hope in MY unfailing love.

Psalm 33:18 (NIV)

Bible Citations

Scripture quotations marked MESSAGE are taken from The Message by Eugene H. Petrson, copyright (c) 1993, 1994, 1995, 1996, 2000, 2001, 2002. Used by permission of NavPress Publishing Group. All rights reserved.

Scripture quotations are from The ESV Bible (The Holy Bible, English Standard Version), copyright 2001 by Crossway, a publishing ministry of Good News Publishers. Used by permission. All rights reserved.

Scripture taken from the Modern English Version (MEV). Copyright 2014 by Military Bible Association. Used by permission. All rights reserved.

BIBLIA SAGRADA – NOVA VERSAO INTERNATIONAL (NIV) 1993, 2000, de International Bible Society

Unless otherwise noted, all Scripture in The Everyday Life Bible is taken from the Amplified BIBLE (AMP) and is used by permission of the Lockman Foundation and the Zondervan Corporation. Additional text copyright 2006

Printed in the United States
by Baker & Taylor Publisher Services

.